BMW MOT S

Doug Mitchel

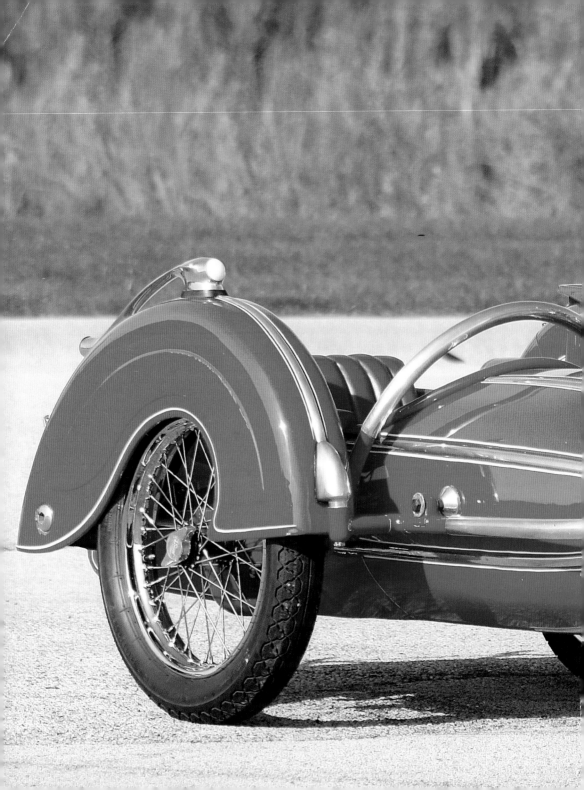

BMW MOTORCYCLES

DOUG MITCHEL

motorbooks

First published in 2015 by Motorbooks, an imprint of Quarto Publishing Group USA Inc., 400 First Avenue North, Suite 400, Minneapolis, MN 55401 USA

Motorbooks titles are also available at discounts in bulk quantity for industrial or sales-promotional use. For details write to Special Sales Manager at Quarto Publishing Group USA Inc., 400 First Avenue North, Suite 400, Minneapolis, MN 55401 USA.

To find out more about our books, visit us online at www.motorbooks.com.

ISBN: 978-0-7603-4798-0

Library of Congress Cataloging-in-Publication Data

Mitchel, Doug.
  BMW motorcycles / Doug Mitchel.
    pages cm
  ISBN 978-0-7603-4798-0 (sc)
  1. BMW motorcycle--History. I. Title.
  TL448.B18M58 2015
  629.227'5--dc23

                 2015002009

Senior Editor: Darwin Holmstrom
Project Manager: Caitlin Fultz
Art Director: Brad Springer
Cover Designer: Matthew Simmons
Layout Designer: Kazuko Collins

On the front cover: 1950 52/2 with Steib S350 sidecar. *Henry von Wartenberg*
On the back cover: 2014 S1000RR, 1976 R90S, 1925 R32
On the title page: 1965 R50/2

Printed in China

10 9 8 7 6 5 4 3 2 1

CONTENTS

In the world of motorcycles, BMW has earned a well-deserved reputation for building a series of machines that seem to last forever. German design and craftsmanship ensures each buyer that the cycle they are about to ride off into the sunset with will serve them well for years to come. As far as history goes, the BMW story is not one of the longest, but has been chock-full of pitfalls and travails, many that threatened the existence of the marque.

In the early years of the 1900s, several manufacturers of motorcycles already were established in the USA alone, as well as many overseas. As soon as someone realized you could create a new brand of motorcycle by bolting a proprietary engine into a frame, every Tom, Dick, and Harry was offering machines that bore their names. Those that survived longer than a week included Thor, Cyclone, and Emblem. Of course Indian began manufacturing motorcycles in 1901 with Harley-Davidson following suit in 1903. There were even a few cycle makers that appeared before 1900, but they came and went, leaving barely a trace. The Daimler name was affixed to something that hinted at a motorcycle, but was not exactly a two-wheeled craft for personal travels. Most of these makers used single-cylinder designs due to the fact that the multicylinder engine for motorcycle use was a few years away from being developed.

The BMW name and company came to be in October 1917, but its main enterprise at that moment was designing and building aircraft engines. Yet once the Treaty of Versailles was signed after the end of World War I, BMW was banned from the production of aircraft engines and was forced to aim its engineering skills elsewhere. To stay afloat, BMW turned its attentions to machinery used on the farm, air brakes used on trains, and casting a variety of products for third-party firms.

In 1920, BMW first started building an engine for use in trucks, a 60-horsepower motor that soon led to additional projects. In 1921, BMW began to produce its M2B15 engine for third-party use in motorcycles. One brand that opted for the powerplant was Victoria, a Munich-based motorcycle builder. That company introduced the R32, its first production motorcycle, at the 1923 Berlin Motor Show.

The R32 carried another flat-twin engine in its flanks, but this time it was transversely mounted with a cylinder seen extending out of both sides of the chassis. The positive response to the R32 gave the young business a new level of confidence, and BMW planned to expand its line of motorcycles, as well as return to the craft of building airplane engines. After post–World War I aircraft manufacturing restrictions were lifted, BMW returned to the assembly and design of high-performance aircraft engines. Some of the manufacturer's earlier aviation designs had won awards for altitude and speed, coveted assets in the world of flight.

As BMW continued to expand its foothold in the motorcycle universe, World War II broke out, hampering its ability to produce anything outside of what was needed for the war. One lucky strike came when the German military sent out a request for a motorcycle designed and built for wartime applications. BMW submitted its plans for the R75 and was

awarded part of the contract. The Zündapp KS75 also won the contract. By building more than 17,000 of the sidecar-equipped R75, BMW kept its name afloat during the war. After World War II ended in 1945, BMW again was faced with the task of trying to stay in business. Its assembly plant at Milbertshofen had been nearly destroyed as a result of Allied bombings, and BMW executives weren't sure if it was worth the effort to rebuild the facility based on the prior demand for motorcycles.

In the end, BMW decided to stay in the motorcycle-making business, and the first postwar models came out in 1948. Actually, one of the reasons the company returned to motorcycle assembly was the anticipated need for low-cost transportation for postwar buyers who needed to get around on something besides their own two feet. Production was slow to get rolling, but BMW was soon back to building its line of high-grade motorcycles for discerning buyers.

It wasn't long after production resumed that BMW noticed a surge in sales in the United States. Returning soldiers provided much of the demand, as many had been given their first taste of cycling during the war. Surplus Harley-Davidson and Indian machines could be purchased for very little money and allowed the ex-GIs to get back into motorcycling for fun this time around. By 1952, BMW had an established stateside presence. Its primary competition was Harley-Davidson, which had not only survived the war but emerged ready and able to produce enough models to satisfy the eager and expanding market in the country. As of 1952, Indian was faltering, and the name was gone (or so we thought) by 1953. A decade later, the Japanese brands were reaching the American shores, adding some real diversity to the market. Most of the early Japanese machines were rudimentary in design and construction but allowed even neophyte riders to get their boots wet in the two-wheeled universe.

BMW began to take notice of the demands that buyers in the United States made before choosing a motorcycle. It appeared that all they wanted was more of everything—more power, speed, comfort, and selection. BMW began to design and produce an ever-wider array of machines. Some claim that BMW went too far from what was considered "normal" or traditional for the Bavarian builder. Inasmuch as that was true, BMW needed to broaden the scope of what it sold in the effort to sell more. It would never achieve the volume levels of the Japanese makers and preferred selling to a client with more refined tastes and who didn't want to be seen on the same model as six of his neighbors. The BMW brand often carries an MSRP that puts it beyond reach of many buyers, but those who could afford the ticket price were rewarded with a finely honed machine that would serve them for decades.

Before too long, the marque had expanded its scope far beyond any of its initial plans back in 1923. The boxer engine was still being produced, but even that fairly standard configuration had undergone extensive revisions to comply with the ongoing demands of buyers. Beyond that, BMW developed three-, four-, and even six-cylinder designs, many of which positively dripped with the latest technology—unlike some other domestic brands that simply dripped. The catalog at your local BMW dealer today is full of everything from behemoth touring models to smaller-scale scooters, but every model in the lineup is produced with the highest level of quality currently available.

As the motorcycle market continues to flex and expand, I'm sure we haven't seen the last of what BMW engineers can dream up and build. I am a big fan of radical new designs, and only the future knows what other levels of technology await us and those who put our two-wheeled dreams into action.

This book takes you through BMW's entire history and shows nearly 40 machines from the pages of the company's history books. We hope you enjoy reading about them as much as you do riding them.

CHAPTER 1

THE PREWAR YEARS

July 20, 1917, marked the first official day of BMW—Bayerische Motoren Werke—becoming a business. But it would take a long and complicated blending of several firms to create the BMW we know today.

In the earliest days, every week brought a new technology or process to the game of manufacturing, regardless of what was being assembled. One of its aircraft engines set a record for vertical climb before further testing was cancelled by the signing of the Treaty of Versailles.

The company had some experience with two-wheeled vehicles prior to building the first BMW motorcycle in 1923. The first example was a small motorized bicycle nicknamed the Flink, which was produced by BFW—Bayerische Flugzeugwerke—one of the companies that became a part of BMW. BFW also built a small motorcycle called the Helios that carried a BMW-manufactured flat-twin cylinder engine longitudinally in its frame. This steppingstone provided valuable insight, and later BMWs would nearly all carry their motors transversely in their frames

BMW's first production motorcycle, the R32, shown at the Berlin Motor Show in 1923, set off waves of excitement within the industrial and motorcycling communities. BMW's technology and standards of quality set the bar a few notches higher than any previous efforts. The 494cc engine produced 8.5 horsepower and enabled the rider to achieve a 56-miles-per-hour top speed. The entire machine weighed only 269 pounds.

BMW quickly gained renown as a builder of high-quality motorcycles, earning the company a dedicated following of riders.

First seen at the Berlin Motor Show in 1923, the R32 represented the abilities of BMW and would lead to many more amazing motorcycles.

Powered by a 494cc, flat-twin engine that delivered 8.5 horsepower at 3,200 rpm, the new ride was a truly capable device. The use of an opposed twin-cylinder motor was not new, but previous makers mounted their engines in line with the frame rails. A single 22mm-carburetor fed the four-stroke design, and a three-speed gearbox was also a part of the layout. A twin-loop frame formed from tubular steel held the opposed twin engine. The 54-inch wheelbase proved stable yet nimble. When topped off with fuel, the R32 tipped the scales at 269 pounds. The angular fuel tank could carry three gallons of fuel, giving the thrifty (80-miles-per-gallon) machine a range of over 200 miles.

Between its debut model year of 1923 and its final production run, 3,090 copies of the R32 rolled off the assembly line. Numerous manufacturers vied for European customers at the time, but the successful R32 secured BMW a place at the table. By building on the original R32 platform, BMW produced a number of fresh models, each with a distinctive form that soon became BMW's signature.

1925 R32

Engine Type: Horizontally opposed twin
Displacement: 494cc
Years Produced: 1923–1926
Valve Configuration: Side valve
Horsepower: 8.5 at 3,200 rpm
Top Speed: 55 miles per hour

Did You Know?

Both Indian and Harley-Davidson offered models powered by opposed-twin-cylinder engines. In contrast to BMW, they placed the motors in line with the frame rails, not transversely.

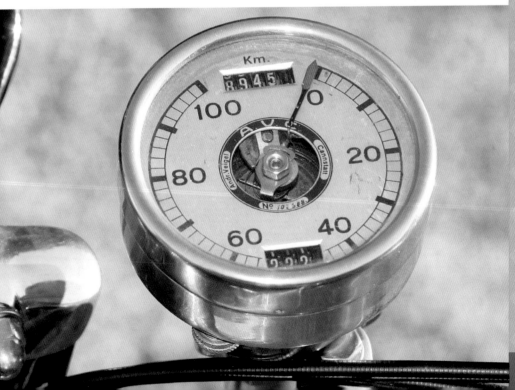

The commercial success of BMW's R32 led to a nearly constant state of change in subsequent models. The R52 arrived as a 1928 model.

The R52 saw several design improvements. The BMW trademark twin-cylinder engine with horizontally opposed jugs had the same horsepower rating—12 at 3,400 rpm—as its predecessor, the R42, but could claim an increase in torque. A single 22mm carburetor kept the twin-cylinder fed, little changed from the R32 design. The transmission still contained three gears, the industry standard of the day. The motor remained

a side-valve design. The ongoing demand for more power pushed displacement to 750cc.

The wheelbase of the R52 was over three-quarters of an inch (0.78) shorter than the R32's wheelbase, but most other physical dimensions remained the same. The fresh R52 had a top speed of 62 miles per hour. An enhanced front-plate spring provided a modicum of front-end suspension while the tail end remained rigid. A solo sprung saddle offered a small amount of added rider comfort for use on roads that had yet to be consistently paved.

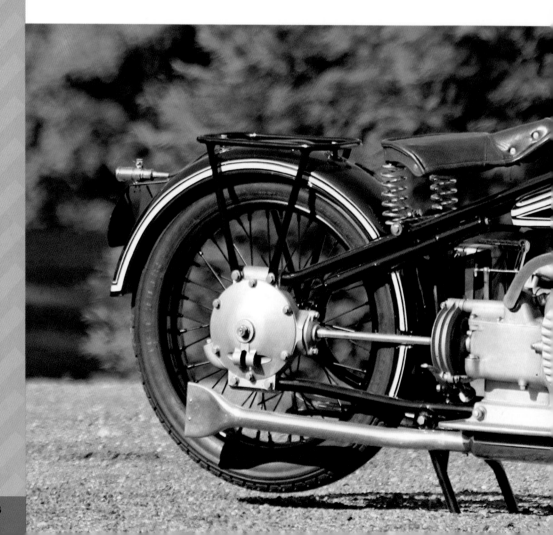

1928 R52

Engine Type: Horizontally opposed twin
Displacement: 486cc
Years Produced: 1928–1929
Valve Configuration: Side valve
Horsepower: 12 at 3,400 rpm
Top Speed: 62 miles per hou

a large increase over the three-year run of the R32. BMW was learning more about production and what the customers demanded with every new motorcycle.

The price of the R52 was almost 700 reichsmarks lower than the R32, pushing R52 sales to 4,377 over two years of production,

Did You Know?

Although the year 1929 marked the beginning of the Great Depression in the United States, BMW remained extremely productive and sold many thousands of bikes during the 1930s.

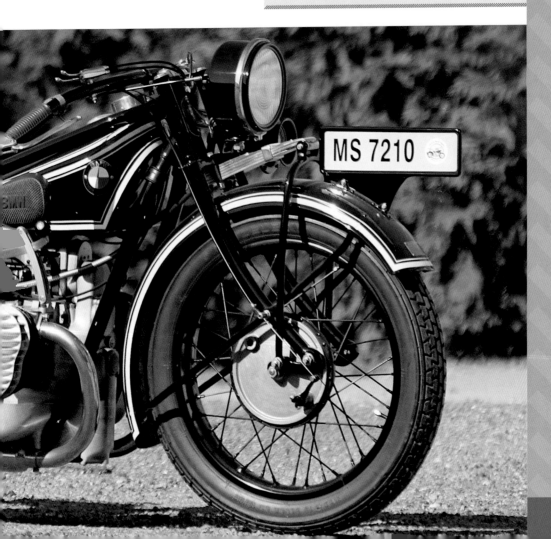

MS 7210

To combat a drop in sales, BMW began to develop less expensive models. Single-cylinder models had been on the BMW roster since 1925, catering to customers who wanted less power but still demanded longevity and dependability.

The R4, introduced in 1932 and displacing 398cc, followed the 1931 R2, a 198cc machine. By using the same platform as the R2 to create the R4, which cost 500 reichsmarks less than the R2, BMW was able to offer a bigger displacement option without reinventing the wheel.

The front fork on the R4 was an enhanced version of the unit used on the R2. Beyond those minor alterations and the doubling of displacement, the R4 was virtually a mirror image of the R2. Production of the R4 ran from 1932 through 1937, and more than 15,000 units were built in that period, most for military use.

1932 R4 SERIES 1

Engine Type: Single-cylinder
Displacement: 398cc
Years Produced: 1932–1937
Valve Configuration: Overhead valve
Horsepower: 12 at 4,000 rpm
Top Speed: 62 miles per hour

Did You Know?

The R4 and R2 were nearly identical in every dimension, save the increased displacement on the R4. Improved front forks and larger fenders were obvious differences between the R4 and its smaller cousin. It also had a right-side kick-start as required by the military.

MS-9989

Making its debut in 1931, the R2 was a motorcycle designed and built to skirt a new German road tax yet still deliver BMW performance. The new law exempted an owner of a cycle that displaced less than 200cc from purchasing a license or paying road taxes. The valvetrain of the 198cc, single-cylinder engine was exposed to the elements for the premier edition, but after 1932 the valvetrain was enclosed for enhanced performance and added durability.

Top speed of the R2 was listed as 59 miles per hour, no mean feat for a cycle of its size. A three-speed gearbox hung off the back of the engine, and expanding drum brakes were found on both ends. From the start, BMW refused to build a cheap motorcycle, and as a result the R2 was not bargain priced despite its reduced

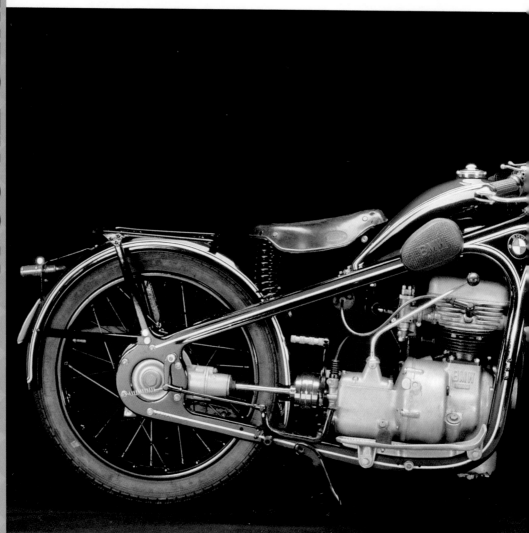

dimensions. The single-cylinder R2 sold for half of what the big twin-cylinder machines sold for but did deliver up to 100 miles per gallon, saving the owner some money over time. During its time of production, which ended in 1936, more than 15,000 copies of the R2 rolled off the assembly line. Every year saw minor improvements. The R2 earned a reputation for being well built, justifying the higher cost.

1933 R2 SERIES 2/33

Engine Type: Single-cylinder
Displacement: 198cc
Years Produced: 1931–1936
Valve Configuration: Overhead valve
Horsepower: 6 at 3,500 rpm
Top Speed: 59 miles per hour

Did You Know?

The R2 was built to capitalize on a German law that exempted riders of motorcycles displacing less than 200cc from purchasing a motorcycle license or having to pay road taxes.

In 1935, BMW made a few changes to its successful R11 model, and the R12 was born. Adding a fourth gear ratio to the transmission and upgrading the front suspension with a telescopic fork greatly improved ride quality and handling. The 745cc, twin-cylinder side-valve engine was fed by either a single 25mm Sum carburetor or a pair of optional 26mm Amal units, which made the R12 a spirited performer. Two additional horsepower were gained by adding the second carb, bringing the total to 20 at 4,000 rpm.

All of the enhancements pushed the weight up to 408 pounds, but the added horsepower offset the added pounds, and the R12 could achieve a top speed of 68 miles per hour, a more than adequate figure for the day. A compact wheelbase of 54.3 inches and low saddle height of 27.5 inches made the powerful R12 easy to handle.

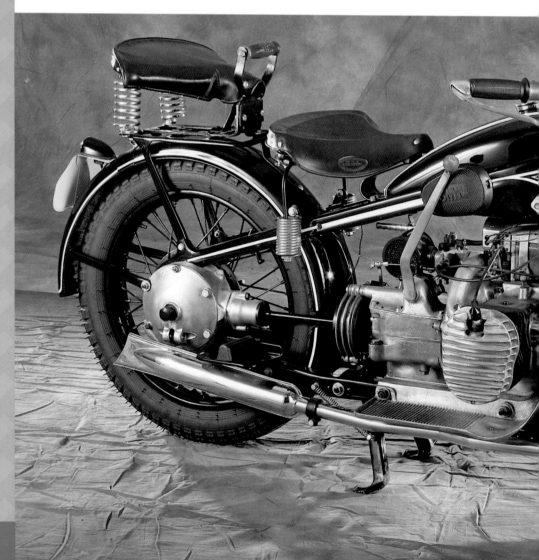

Another reason for the R12's success was the fairly low cost of entry: $388 in US dollars in 1935. The most expensive Harley-Davidson of 1935 cost $347 but lacked many of the high-tech features of the R12. Production of the R12 ran until 1942, when World War II forced production of civilian vehicles to be reduced to the absolute minimum so that precious commodities could be used for the war effort.

1935 R12

Engine Type: Horizontally opposed twin
Displacement: 745cc
Years Produced: 1935–1942
Valve Configuration: Side valve
Horsepower: 18 at 3,400 with single carb, 20 at 4,000 with dual carbs
Top Speed: 68 miles per hour single carb, 74 mph twin carb

Did You Know?

BMW created the R12 by adding a four-speed gearbox and telescopic front fork to the R11. These two upgrades improved the ride and handling to a high degree.

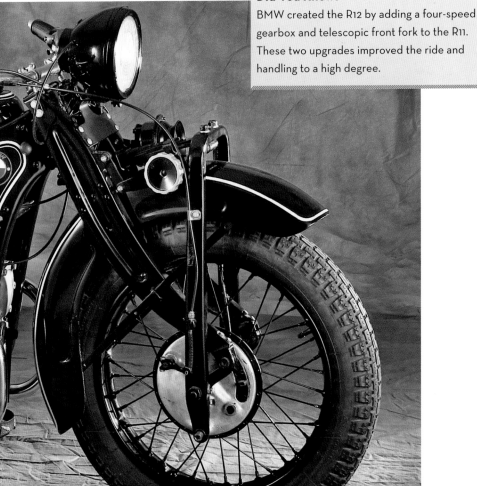

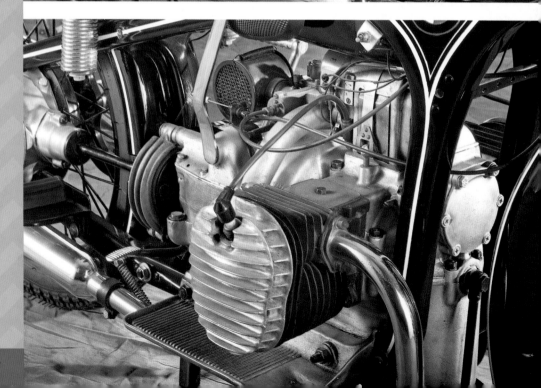

Soon after BMW began building motorcycles, the company began to race them at sanctioned venues. The Bavarian machines proved to be worthy adversaries, and BMW racked up an impressive number of wins in a short period of time. This reign began in the latter part of the 1920s and continued into the early 1930s, when the competition fielded competitive machines and ended BMW's dominance. This didn't sit well with the factory, and steps were taken to return BMW to its former racing glory.

The easiest way to achieve that was to find more power. Supercharging added enormous horsepower, so BMW bolted a supercharger to its 492cc, flat-twin motor, creating the Kompressor. BMW soon returned to racing dominance.

The Kompressor also featured bevel-driven overhead camshafts. The Dell'Orto carburetor on this example was fitted with an enormous velocity stack to direct oxygen into the engine.

The war put racing on the back burner. When it ended, BMW and many other factories returned to the track to compete again.

1938 KOMPRESSOR

Engine Type: Horizontally opposed twin
Displacement: 492cc
Years Produced: 1935–1939
Valve Configuration: Overhead cam
Horsepower: 55
Top Speed: N/A

Did You Know?

In 1951, the use of superchargers on racing motorcycles was banned, so the Kompressor's was removed for racing.

When the German army needed motorcycles, BMW was chosen to supply them. The K75 was a Zündapp R75 BMW, a larger model for use with a sidecar. The R12 was for lighter duty use and primarily carried soldiers to and from a point of action.

Changes to the R12 civilian version permitted easier use for soldiers wearing battle gear. The footpegs were supplanted by a pair of aluminum foot boards that more easily accommodated a pair of heavy-duty boots, which were often covered in mud. The solo saddle was joined by a secondary pillion to carry another soldier to and from his location.

1939 R12 & R12 MILITARY

Engine Type: Horizontally opposed twin
Displacement: 745cc
Years Produced: 1938–1942
Valve Configuration: Side valve
Horsepower: 18 at 3,400 rpm
Top Speed: 68 miles per hour

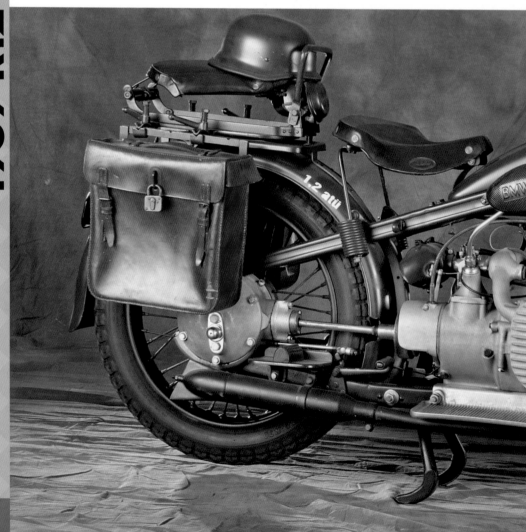

Leather saddlebags were hung over the rear fender to accommodate any additional gear that needed to be carried into action. Leather straps and padlocks kept the contents secure. The shaft drive proved to be far more durable than belt or chain drives were, especially when things got dirty and wet.

The resulting combination of user-friendly features and the dependable drivetrain made the BMW a popular machine. The German military ordered tens of thousands of them.

Did You Know?
Harley-Davidson was commissioned by the US government to design a different motorcycle to handle the demands of operating in the desert. The XA was built for that purpose and used an opposed-twin engine that was very similar to BMW's design. Only 1,000 were produced, and very few remain intact today.

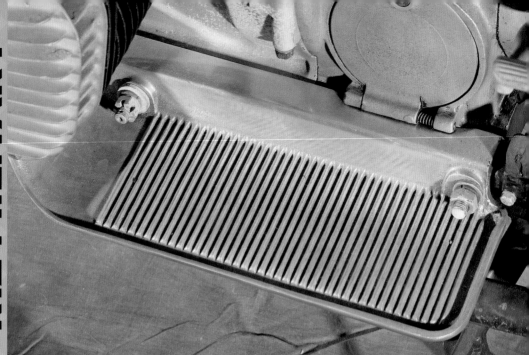

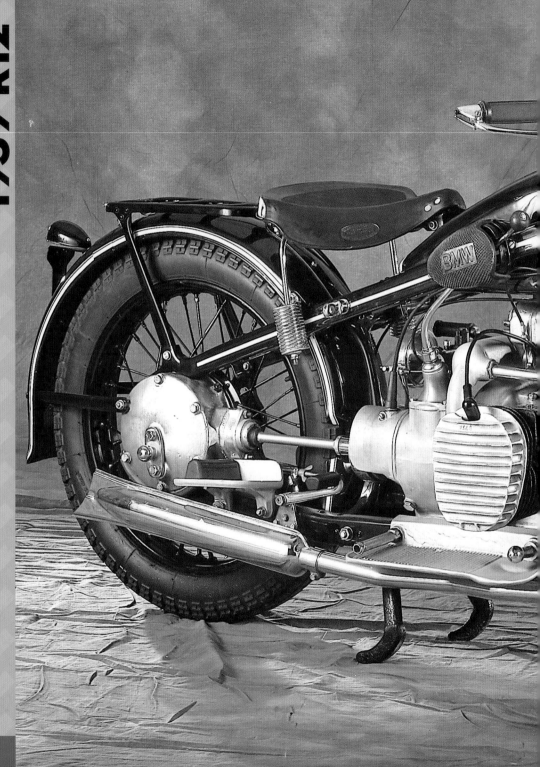

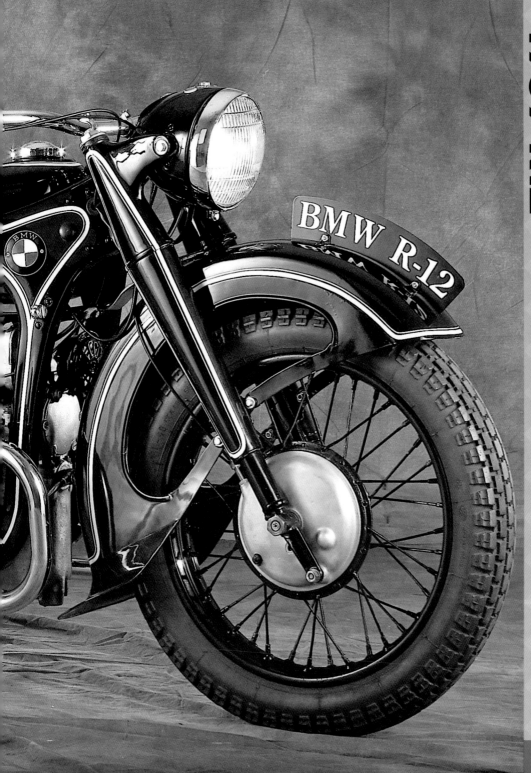

When World War II began in September of 1939, the armies of the world needed transportation. By 1939, BMW was capable of building almost any design asked of the manufacturer. When the Wehrmacht provided specifications for a sidecar-equipped machine, BMW was ready.

BMW opted to improve on the R71's motor to better meet the military's demands. Choosing a 745cc opposed-twin design, the company developed its newest model, the R75. Able to crawl at low speeds for hours, as well as handle rough terrain at high speed, the R75 could be equipped with a wide variety of armament, including the Mauser MG34, a nonfunctioning version of which is attached to the rig pictured here.

One unique feature of the R75 was the attachment of the sidecar, which also provided power to the wheel on the hack. The drivetrain was composed of a high-ratio gearbox that included a reverse gear on the engine as well as another on the differential. For normal conditions, the gearbox offered four forward

and one reverse gear. Off-road conditions limited forward ratios to three. The frames of the R75 and its matched sidecar were stout and capable of standing up to any challenge presented. A trio of drum brakes, one on each wheel, handled stopping duties.

Before the R75 was loaded with a weapon, fuel cans, and two riders, it weighed 800 pounds. The engine delivered 26 horsepower, which was barely enough to get the armed behemoth moving, but once in motion it was a formidable force on three wheels. Nearly

18,000 R75s were produced for wartime use between 1941 and 1944. In 1945, World War II ended, and like many other manufacturers in Europe, BMW would need some time to get back into the business of producing its two-wheeled machines.

1942 R75 MILITARY WITH SIDECAR

Engine Type: Horizontally opposed twin
Displacement: 745cc
Years Produced: 1941–1944
Valve Configuration: Overhead valve
Horsepower: 26 at 4,000 rpm
Top Speed: 59 miles per hour

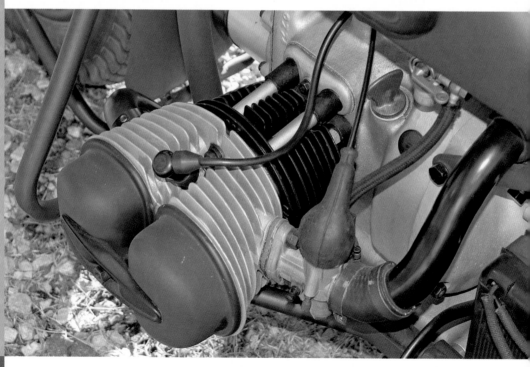

Did You Know?

As the war was drawing to a close, Hitler demanded that any functioning production facilities be destroyed so as not to fall into the Allied forces' hands. Luckily for BMW, its Milbertshofen assembly plant was spared further damage, allowing production to begin again after the war.

CHAPTER 2
POSTWAR, PRE-USA

The years that led up to the end of World War II saw a nonstop deluge of news from the front and the ramped-up production of munitions and other gear. It wasn't long after the cessation that those on both sides of the world could now begin to rebuild. Complications on several fronts would hamper BMW's return to production, some of which came from within company ranks. Some BMW executives weren't sure that restarting motorcycle production was worth the effort required, but BMW chose to begin production as soon as its infrastructure was up to the task.

Another facet of the equation was that BMW was legally banned from producing their previous product lines until 1948.

The first of BMW's postwar machines was the R24, which made its debut at the Geneva Motor Show in 1948. Based on the R23, the latest entrant featured many cues borrowed from the R75. Production began in the latter part of 1948 and rolled on through 1950, with a total of more than 12,000 copies heading off to European dealers.

As BMW continued to develop its markets and machines, it introduced the R52 as a replacement for the R24 in 1950. Sold from 1951 to 1956, more than 100,000 rolled off the assembly lines.

Even bigger news for 1950 was the triumphant return of the boxer twin engine. This newest iteration, based on the prewar R51, was labeled the R51/2, in keeping with BMW's format for model-line progression.

Meanwhile, BMW was closely watching motorcycle sales in the United States and how enthusiastically American buyers were riding home a variety of European and American brands and figured there was room for a new face in the crowd.

As BMW continued to regain its footing after the war, the manufacturer found that by upgrading previous models it could keep the product line fresh enough to attract new buyers and have some previous customers return for a newer version of their favorite machines. In keeping with BMW's method of indicating a new version of a carryover model, the R51 became the R51/2. The "slash" device worked well for BMW and its growing arena of fans. In modern terms, the /2 was the equivalent of the 2.0 designation for software.

BMW chose to upgrade its R51 based on the model's prewar success. The horizontally opposed layout had served BMW well prior to the war as well as during it, and the R75 sidecar unit was used in high numbers during the conflict. One carryover feature of the wartime R75 seen on the R51/2 was the split valve covers. The redesign suited the street-bound version well. The R51/2 was still powered by a flat-twin 494cc engine that delivered 24 horsepower at 5,800 rpm. The fuel tank had a three-gallon capacity, which limited your travels unless refueling was an easy option. A pair of Bing carbs meted out the fuel needed with ease. Slowing the R51/2 was a drum brake at each wheel, each measuring 7 7/8 inches. With a

wet weight of 408 pounds sans rider, the R51/2 was not a lightweight, nor overly awkward. A reasonable saddle height of 29 inches made it easy for a rider to perform low-speed maneuvers and park the R51/2.

The choice of four gears on the R51/2 allowed the rider to reduce rpm at highway speeds. The bike could reach an 83-mile-per-hour top speed, making the R51/2 a favorite among gentleman riders. It was not terribly hasty or ill-tempered, and had just enough power to get you to your next polo match or other respectable engagement with no stress from your mount.

Offered from 1950 to 1951, the R51/2 had a production run of 5,000 units. The radically enhanced R51/3 hit triple digits for its run from 1951 to 1954, but BMW had begun selling its wares in the United States as of 1952, radically expanding its market.

1950 R51/2

Engine Type: Horizontally opposed twin
Displacement: 494cc
Years Produced: 1950–1951
Valve Configuration: Overhead valve
Horsepower: 24 at 5,800 rpm
Top Speed: 83 miles per hour

Did You Know?

With the exception of the 745cc twin used in the wartime R75, BMW did not use a boxer engine in its machines from 1942 until 1944. The reduced availability of many raw materials, as well as paying customers, forced BMW to reduce costs to continue building and selling motorcycles as the war raged on.

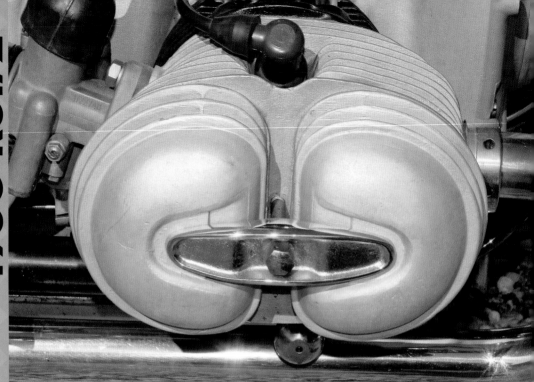

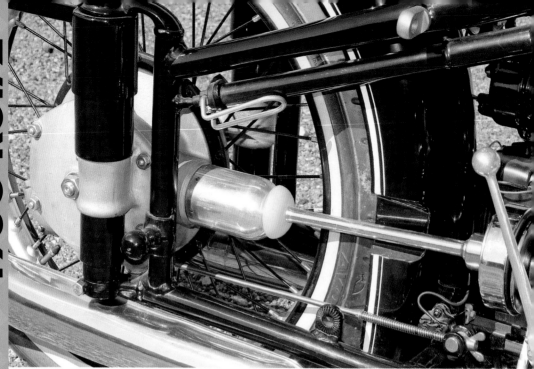

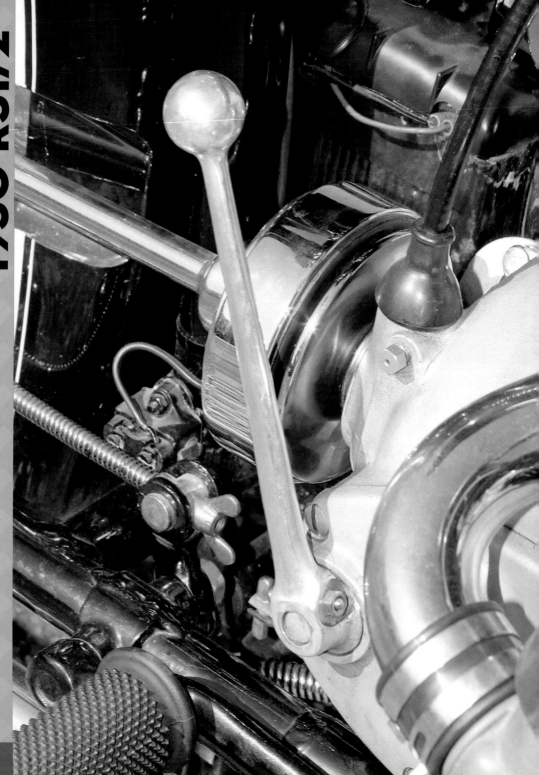

CHAPTER 3

WELCOME TO AMERICA

In 1952 BMW set up its first US dealership. The company had finally recovered enough to sell directly to the vast market in the Unites States. In 1954, Butler & Smith became the sole importer in the United States.

The arrival of BMW predated the Japanese onslaught by about a decade, and the only real competition for the Bavarian motorcycle maker was from Harley-Davidson. By 1952, the other primary builder from the United States, Indian, was on the verge of being sold and discontinuing motorcycle sales (for now). Triumph, Norton, Moto Guzzi, and BSA were still surviving and producing motorcycles in the early 1950s, but their struggles would also intensify as soon as Honda and the like arrived on American shores.

Both the styling and mechanical design of the BMW motorcycles now being sold directly in the United States were pure German, with no features that didn't find a useful place on the machine. BMW offered a limited color palette of black, white, and some red models, each hue with pinstripes of a contrasting shade. The company continued to push its existing line of machines using its slash system to classify its various editions. The time-tested boxer motor was still the primary powerplant offered by BMW, with a variety of iterations coming in the decades to follow. The horizontally opposed cylinders produced a decent amount of horsepower, along with ample torque to handle nearly any style of riding on the streets of the United States. Two single-cylinder models remained in the catalog until 1966 and then were gone for many years. Between 1952 and 1970, BMW didn't have any radical changes in its designs or technology, but when the early to mid-1970s came, that would change.

Following in the tire tracks of the R25/3, the R26 made its debut as a 1956 model and carried several important upgrades to the single-cylinder entrant. Horsepower in the R26 was up to 15 at 6,400 rpm, a boost of two ponies. This increase was the result of installing a bigger 26mm carb in the R26. A paper air cleaner helped the R26 breath better, which was also a power benefit. Larger cooling fins on the single-cylinder mill assisted in keeping the more powerful R26 cool and made identifying the motorcycle easy when seen next to other models from BMW.

Improved suspension on the R26 did its part to enhance handling and ride quality, both of which were a concern for the new sea of American buyers. Without any fuel in its four-gallon tank, the R26 weighed less than 350 pounds and was capable of reaching

79 miles per hour at its peak. All of the upgrades on the R26 allowed it to sell as well as anything else in this period of diminished cycle sales in most parts of the world. Exports to Third World countries, as well as to the United States, kept production figures at less than 5,000 for the premier year. When the R26 was discontinued in 1960, more than 30,000 had been sold.

1956 R26

Engine Type: Single-cylinder
Displacement: 247cc
Years Produced: 1956–1960
Valve Configuration: Overhead valve
Horsepower: 15 at 6,400 rpm
Top Speed: 79 miles per hour

Did You Know?

When the BMW R26 was introduced in 1956, Harley-Davidson's KH and KHK models were being phased out, leaving room for H-D's brand-new model, the Sportster. That model series was named the XL and was a smaller variant in the Harley catalog, much like the R26.

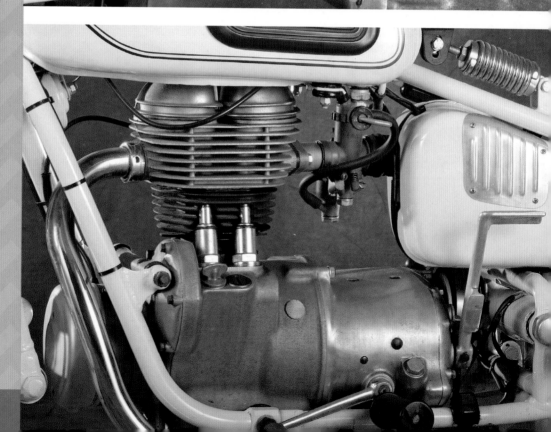

BMW introduced two new models, the R60 and R69, at the Brussels Motor Show in January of 1955, even as the motorcycle industry was suffering from poor sales. Both of these fresh faces were based on prior designs and hardware but had upgrades to the powerplants and suspension systems. Both of the new models came fitted with the unique Earles front forks and enhanced rear suspensions.

1958 R69

Engine Type: Horizontally opposed twin
Displacement: 594cc
Years Produced: 1955–1960
Valve Configuration: Overhead valve
Horsepower: 35 at 6,800 rpm
Top Speed: 102 miles per hour

The R69 borrowed its 594cc engine from the R68. This powerplant already had a proven record for output and reliability. Adding the latest suspension to both ends made for an appealing package that was suited for a wide variety of riding styles. The R69 also had a revamped gearbox and clutch, making both easier for riders to use.

Once underway, the R69 could reach a top speed of just over 100 miles per hour, and with a filled 4.1-gallon tank, it weighed 445 pounds. Output for the R69 was the same as it had been in the R68, giving the rider a maximum of 35 horsepower at 6,800 rpm. This came as no surprise, since the engine was a direct carryover from the previous R68 model. The four-speed gearbox had become the standard for BMW transmissions. Each wheel had a 7 7/8-inch drum brake, and, as expected, a shaft drive provided the required connection from gearbox to rear sprocket.

In spite of the improved features, sales of R69 motorcycles remained poor for a couple of years. During its five-year run, only 2,956 R69s were produced. Company-wide, a total of only 15,500 motorcycles were produced in 1956, and the following year a paltry 5,429 rolled off the lines. BMW was not the only name suffering from low sales, but that wasn't much consolation to the Bavarian bike builder.

Did You Know?
Even the mighty Harley-Davidson was experiencing a downturn in the mid-1950s, and fewer than 7,000 examples of their 1955 models were produced.

In the three years leading up to the release of its 1960 models, BMW found itself in a poor financial situation; one of its rivals, Mercedes-Benz, was eyeing a takeover of the hurting motorcycle and automotive manufacturer. Among BMWs supporters was Herbert Quandt, a banker who was not fond of the swiftly approaching absorption by Mercedes. Quandt rallied his contacts and raised enough funds to stave off the merger and keep the BMW name moving ahead under its own power. Sales of the company's newest car, the

1961 R50S

Engine Type: Horizontally opposed twin
Displacement: 494cc
Years Produced: 1960–1962
Valve Configuration: Overhead valve
Horsepower: 35 at 7,650 rpm
Top Speed: 99.4 miles per hour

700—launched in 1959 and powered by one of BMW's boxer motorcycle engines—thankfully boosted the company's bottom line and helped keep it afloat as an independent firm.

More success followed in 1960, when BMW introduced four new motorcycle models, its first new offerings since 1956. Among them, the R50S was equipped with some hot-rod hardware that boosted performance and, as a result, sales. The R50S featured BMW's already-popular 494cc boxer engine but had high-compression pistons and a more aggressive cam than previous models. To feed the new design, larger 26mm carburetors were mounted to the cylinders. As a result of these tweaks, horsepower was upped to 35 at 7,650 rpm—an impressive figure at the time. Assisting the R50S in getting its newfound power to the street was a close-ratio gearbox with four speeds at the rider's disposal.

The example pictured here is finished in Bristol Gray, which was a BMW automotive hue. At the time this one was built, anyone who could come up with a 10-bike order could select any of the colors in the BMW catalog to be applied to the batch. This 1961 edition came complete with a Hella spotlight/mirror combination and a cam-driven tachometer. The swinging rear pillion was not intended for a passenger; it gave the rider's posterior a more useful location to rest while he twisted the throttle to wide open and put the R50S through its paces. This example also features Denfeld leather saddlebags.

The R50S was only produced until the 1962 model year, and in that time, only 1,634 came off company lines, making them a rare sight today.

Did You Know?

As of 1958, European makers had only each other as competition, but in 1959, Honda arrived in the United States. As soon as Honda opened its first dealer showroom, people from all walks of life began hitting the streets aboard a machine from the Japanese upstart.

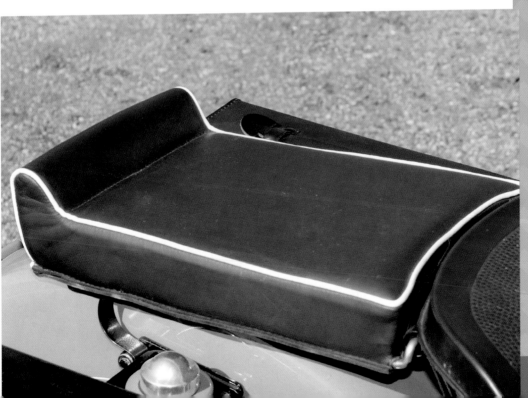

The premier edition of the R50 was introduced in 1955 and proved itself to be a worthy machine for riders of nearly any stripe. It even could be ridden with a sidecar attached for added family fun. During its five-year run, more than 13,000 copies were produced; some headed stateside, since BMW had opened up shop in the United States in 1952.

For 1960, the R50 gained a /2 designation, and sales continued to notch even higher. The 494cc boxer engine continued to produce 26 horsepower at 5,800 rpm, as the R50s had. A four-speed gearbox with foot shifter was also a carryover from the previous iteration. The design remained workable with or without a sidecar, and when buyers opted to add a sidecar, they most often chose a Steib attachment. Both R50/2s shown here are from 1965, and the owners opted for different setups for use. The aluminum handle on the fender of the sidecar-equipped version is known as the "cobra," due to its contours that very much mimic

the basket-dwelling snake. The hard-sided saddlebags on the other example allow the rider and a passenger to carry enough for a weekend away, especially if headed to a nudist's camp, judging by the somewhat cramped space within the walls of the shapely bags.

The R50/2 stayed in production until 1969. More than 19,000 headed to buyers around the globe. As the saying goes, if it ain't broke, don't fix it, and the R50 and R50/2 variant are perfect examples of that adage.

1965 R50/2

Engine Type: Horizontally opposed twin
Displacement: 494cc
Years Produced: 1960–1969
Valve Configuration: Overhead valve
Horsepower: 26 at 5,800 rpm
Top Speed: 87 miles per hour (no sidecar); 62 miles per hour (sidecar)

Did You Know?

Honda began selling motorcycles in the United States in 1959, and very quickly other American and European manufacturers noticed the impact. That only intensified when Kawasaki, Suzuki, and Yamaha arrived on American shores.

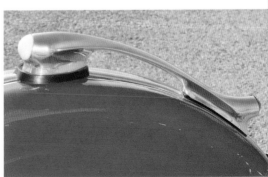

BMW's early production machines all had a single-cylinder engine in the frame. The design and mechanical simplicity of the powerplant made them appealing, even though they lacked the power of some multicylinder models on the market. The R23 first was introduced in 1938 and also was the first to use the 247cc displacement. The R23 sold decently and was later supplanted by the R24, R25, and R26. BMW was always careful to mark its model lineage in an easy-to-follow format—thus the single-digit change in model number over the years.

The 1960 R27 proved to be the final version of the venerable single-cylinder machine. The high cost and low power output restricted the size of the buyers' market, and by 1960 the models, power, and variation being delivered by the Japanese manufacturers made it difficult for BMW to continue with a single-cylinder model, especially with a machine that had made its entrance into the market more than two decades earlier.

The layout and output had varied only slightly in the years before 1966, and even those upgrades did little to keep pace with the other cycles being introduced. The 247cc engine delivered 18 horsepower at 7,400 rpm, shifted through a four-speed gearbox. Tipping the scales at 357 pounds when fueled, the R27 only had a four-gallon tank, again not making it a top choice for buyers. Top speed without a sidecar was 80.8 miles per hour; the R27 only hit 55.9 miles per hour when encumbered. A pair of average size (6 19/64-inch diameter) drum brakes were able to slow the R27 down, as long as you had plenty of space before becoming one with the obstacle in front of you.

Members of the media who tested the R27 spoke fairly about it in their reviews, but by telling the truth and nothing but the truth, they caused the model to fall short of sales expectations. The R27 and its predecessors had served the market well, but that market was shrinking by the hour. As a result, the R27 was removed from BMW's roster in 1966.

1966 R27

Engine Type: Single-cylinder
Displacement: 247cc
Years Produced: 1960–1966
Valve Configuration: Overhead valve
Horsepower: 18 at 7,400 rpm
Top Speed: 80.8 (no sidecar), 55.9 (with sidecar)

Did You Know?

In 1966, the Japanese motorcycle invasion all but erased sales from other makers, save Triumph, and when Honda introduced the CB750 in 1969, the entire two-wheeled world changed, forever.

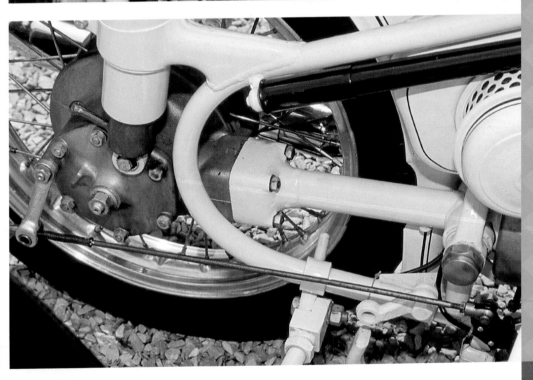

BMW began selling its wares in the United States in 1952. Before the company took the plunge, however, those at BMW could anticipate the impact a market this large would have on the maker's bottom line. Once the machines began to arrive, the US consumer was curious but only semi-eager. So sales were okay but not life sustaining. In particular, potential buyers complained about the Earles forks BMW used on every model of motorcycle. This was part of a time-tested design that worked well but was unlike anything seen on any other motorcycle in the United States.

1969 R60US

Engine Type: Horizontally opposed twin
Displacement: 594cc
Years Produced: 1967–1969
Valve Configuration: Overhead valve
Horsepower: 30 at 5,800 rpm
Top Speed: 90 miles per hour

In an effort to garner more sales, BMW chose to create models specifically for American sales and used a traditional telescopic front fork in lieu of the Earles. Three different machines were introduced, and their model identifications

made BMW's intentions obvious. The R50US, R60US, and R69US all came equipped with the fork design that American buyers recognized, and sales increased slightly. The revised front suspension was not meant to be a game changer but was a way to quell the complaints from potential buyers until the next round of fresh models could be crafted by BMW engineers.

The R60US sported the same hardware as the R60, except the newer version had contemporary shocks up front. The 594cc boxer motor was still at home in the double-loop steel tubular frame that was a mainstay of the BMW template. The frames on the US versions were also devoid of sidecar mounting lugs, as sales of sidecar-equipped models were almost nonexistent. Many magazine reviews simultaneously cheered and scorned the BMW as a dependable machine with a frame that withstood the test of time. The critics weren't always kind in their choice of vocabulary, as the configuration was rather staid and heavier than it should have been, mainly because the chassis was designed to be attached to a sidecar. With the fuel tank topped off to its four-gallon capacity, the R60US weighed 430 pounds. It could reach a top speed of 90 miles per hour and carried a pair of 7 7/8-inch-diameter drum brakes assigned to slow the heavy R60US to a halt.

Built from 1967 through 1969, the R60US was successful when it came to sales. The next range of models from BMW would need to up the ante in order to maintain and expand the pool of buyers on this side of the pond.

Did You Know?

The creation of its US models helped BMW gain some traction on American soil, but at the end of the lifespan of those models, the team at Honda was ready to unleash its world-changing model: the CB750. BMW's challenge to sell in the United States would grow more daunting—as did the chances of any other motorcycle maker—unless they could create a cycle that could compete with the CB750.

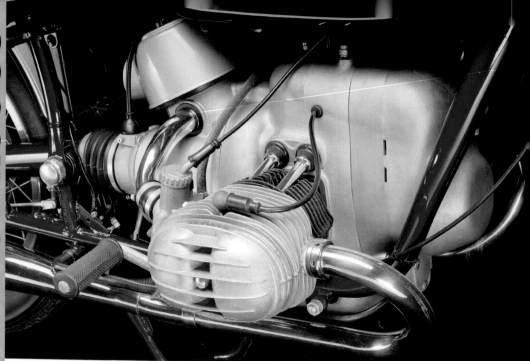

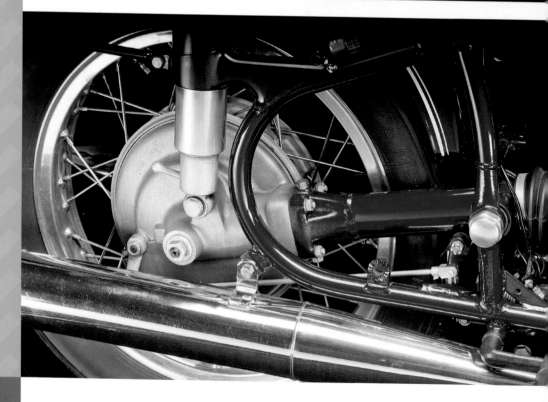

More than a decade after introducing its unique style of motorcycles in the United States on a large scale, BMW was still trying to find the best way to attract more American buyers to its models. Twin-cylinder engines weren't rare in the motorcycle world, but the opposed-twin design was all BMW. Mechanically, it was a fine design that lasted much longer than some other configurations, but it was far from exciting. Dependable, durable, and long-lasting, yes— thrilling, no. The release of the R75/5 tried to throw a bit of gas onto the fire. Making its debut as a 1969 model, the R75/5 set the tone for BMWs for the next few years.

Although still employing the traditional BMW opposed-twin layout, the R75/5 brought new levels of sophistication and technology to the game. The result was a machine that retained traits coveted by loyal BMW riders but offered new technology and traits never before seen on the earlier stodgy Bavarian models.

At the core, the R75/5 carried its 745cc engine in a radical (for BMW) frame. In addition to its highly revised frame design, the R75/7 addressed fuel delivery, electrics, breathing, and horsepower in a single model.

Feeding the bigger mill were a pair of 32mm Bing carburetors with concentric float bowls. A bevy of other upgrades pushed the output of the 745cc engine to 57 horsepower at 6,400 rpm, an unheard-of figure on a street-legal BMW. When fully laden with 6.1 gallons of fuel, the R75/5

weighed in at 436 pounds, which was respectable for a machine of its size. At full power, the R75/5 could hit 103 miles per hour, another figure not seen on a BMW in previous editions.

The R75/5's production ended in 1973, and the machines that followed used it as inspiration as BMW grew more attractive to demanding US buyers.

1969 R75/5

Engine Type: Horizontally opposed twin
Displacement: 745cc
Years Produced: 1969–1973
Valve Configuration: Overhead valve
Horsepower: 57 at 6,400 rpm
Top Speed: 103 miles per hour

Did You Know?

In 1969, both the BMW R75/5 and Honda CB750/4 debuted. Despite the fact that the machines had few similarities, their specs weren't too far apart. The Honda delivered more power yet weighed 60 pounds more. It also could reach a higher top speed yet sold for $200 less than the latest BMW. Different strokes for different folks never rang so true.

CHAPTER 4

THE 1970s "R" HERE

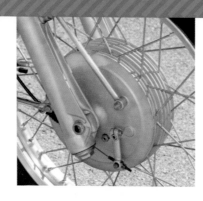

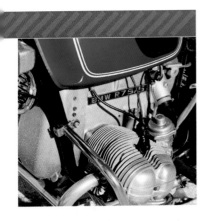

By 1972, BMW had been selling its motorcycles in the United States for twenty years. The company was able to put the dismal sales of the 1960s behind it and restart its previous evolution of models in the 1970s. The family tree had never been one of daring or provocative alterations, and until 1983 only variants of the R models were seen in BMW's sales catalogs. This didn't hinder options for buyers, as several different models could be ridden home from the growing network of dealers across the United States.

The 1972 listings featured BMWs wearing revised four-gallon fuel tanks along with saddles that provided passengers with a different style of grab rails for added comfort. The new R90S debuted in 1973, with a new level of performance and a more aggressive appearance. Another classic model was the R100RS, which first appeared in 1976. Several additional designs made their debut in this period and were fitted with a wide variety of engine displacements, but all would retain the horizontally opposed, twin-cylinder configuration until the 1983 editions appeared.

Throughout the 1970s, the BMW brand of motorcycles gained steam and was not overshadowed by the sales of its automotive siblings. There had been a stretch that nearly forced the two-wheeled BMW machines into retirement until cooler heads prevailed. Because of demands from US buyers, some exciting designs from BMW would be coming soon.

Of the three new /5 models that made their debut in 1969, the R60/5 was in the middle of these models' power range with its 599cc engine. Every one of the new models was built with a revised frame and an all-alloy engine that featured the camshaft beneath the crankshaft and a four-speed gearbox. An electric starter was standard on the R60/5 and R75/5 and was an option on the R50/5. It was a feature that added value and ease of use to the brand. In keeping with buyers seeking more performance from their rides, the latest /5 models were not built with frames ready for sidecar use. This saved weight and complexity, adding to the sporty nature. Additional weight-saving moves brought the tonnage down to a svelte 463 pounds. The reduced weight and output of 40 horsepower at 6,400 rpm gave the R60/5 uplifting performance.

1972 R60/5

Engine Type: Horizontally opposed twin
Displacement: 599cc
Years Produced: 1969–1973
Valve Configuration: Overhead valve
Horsepower: 40 at 6,400 rpm
Top Speed: 103.7 miles per hour

In 1972, for a dash of style, four-gallon "toaster" fuel tanks made their debut. The chrome side panels reminded people of the kitchen appliance of the same name, making it an easy way to ID the '72s. The last year of the /5 was 1973, and further revisions brought more buyers to BMW.

The /5 models were the first series to be completely assembled at BMW's new Berlin facility. The Munich plant had been retooled for automotive assembly, moving employees skilled in motorcycle assembly to the new location, which was now ready for action. BMW's 1970/5 model production totaled 12,287, and by the end of /5 production, nearly 69,000 had been built. Sales of the German marque was growing by leaps and bounds, with decades of continued acceleration to follow.

Did You Know?

Production of the R60/5 reached 22,721 in its five-year run, which was a vast improvement over that of previous models from BMW. The Berlin factory exclusively produced motorcycles, making it far simpler to ramp up assembly as required.

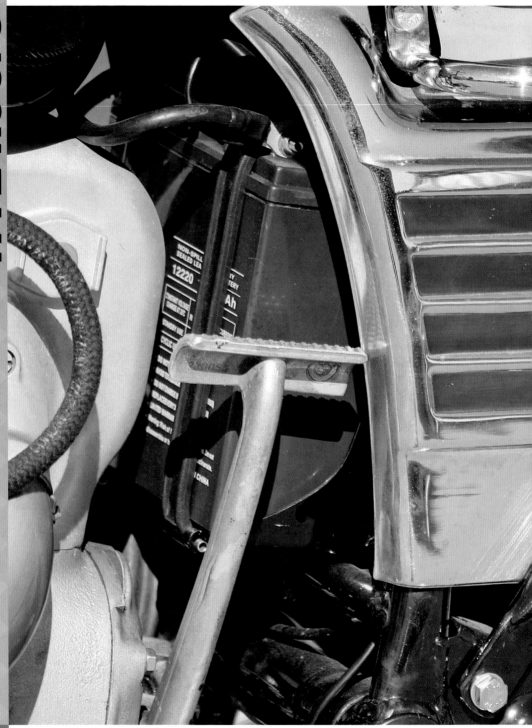

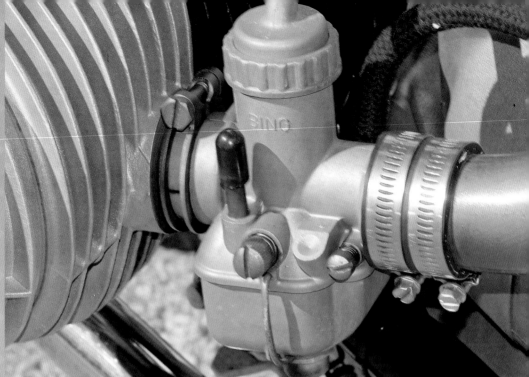

Of the /5 models debuting in 1969, the R75 was at the top of the food chain. It carried a 745cc, twin-cylinder engine in its revised frame and was mated to a four-speed gearbox. The larger displacement engine had the same configuration as the smaller variants in the /5 family, which had the camshaft above the

1973 R75/5

Engine type: Horizontally opposed twin
Displacement: 745cc
Years Produced: 1969–1973
Valve Configuration: Overhead valve
Horsepower: 50 at 6,200 rpm
Top Speed: 108 miles per hour

crank. A pair of 32mm Bing carbs fed the more powerful engine with ease, and the big /5 hit a velocity of 108 miles per hour. The R75/5 could be equipped with a 4.7- or 6-gallon fuel tank, and they were interchangeable. The biggest /5 weighed the same as its smaller R60/5 brethren at 463 pounds. The electric start was another feature found on all of the /5 models except the R50/5, and 1975 was the last year a kick-start lever appeared on a BMW boxer motorcycle. (The kick-start remained an option after 1975.)

The Mint Green example seen here is a European spec model for 1973. Euro models sported a five-speed gearbox, as well as several additional unique features. The fuel tank was larger than the US version, the bars were lower for a more race-oriented approach, and more paint options were on tap. The front fender was fitted with a vertical license plate, but that was omitted for use on the streets of the United States.

Production of the R75/5 totaled 38,370 in its complete history, a number that was an indicator of improving conditions in the world of motorcycling.

Did You Know?

The success of the BMW /5 series paved the way for the debut of one of the most legendary models of all time, the R90S, which made its premier appearance as a 1974 model. The /5s were discontinued after the 1973 model year ended.

Robust sales of the /5 models paved the way for one of BMW's more daring designs to debut in 1974: the R90S. This model would push the German maker into the rarified air of the Japanese superbikes that were coming into focus. Although still powered by the traditional boxer engine, the R90S had added power and revolutionary design elements. Hans Muth created the design; later his work would encompass Japanese machines as well as subsequent BMW entries. The bikini fairing up front was the most obvious upgrade, and behind

1975 & 1976 R90S

Engine Type: Horizontally opposed twin
Displacement: 898cc
Years Produced: 1973–1976
Valve Configuration: Overhead valve
Horsepower: 67 at 7,000 rpm
Top Speed: 124 miles per hour

it was a concise instrument panel fitted with a nice array of gauges. The fairing, fuel tank, and tail section added up to a streamlined look that was accented by two-tone paint schemes. Your

1975

choice of the Smoke Silver or Daytona Orange palettes were adorned with adhesive pinstripes, displacing the previous hand-painted trim.

A pair of Dell'Orto 38mm carbs fed the 898cc boxer twin, and the sporty entry touted 67 horsepower at 7,000 rpm. An extra gear ratio brought the total to five, another first for the German maker. A pair of disc brakes were installed at the front wheel. It was an advancement found on the R90S that helped the machine slow down from its top speed of 124 miles per hour. The 1974 edition brakes were not drilled, unlike the 1975 and 1976 versions.

The focused intentions of the R90S kept its sales from reaching new heights in its three years of production. The premier edition carried an MSRP of $3,430, almost twice the cost of any of the Japanese sport machines of the same period. The low production figures have made the R90S one of BMW's most coveted collector models.

Did You Know?
Hans Muth was credited with designing both the R90S and an even more radical machine, the Katana, sold by Suzuki in 1982 and 1983.

1975

1975

1975

1976

1976

1976

For 1977, the R90S grew in displacement and was seen in two forms, the R100S and RS. The new RS wore several unique styling cues, as well as a modified rear-end ratio that compensated for the full fairing. The RS moniker referred to the German word *Rennsport*, "racing" (see Did You Know), and the model was considered

1977 R100RS

Engine Type: Horizontally opposed twin
Displacement: 980cc
Years Produced: 1976–1984
Valve Configuration: Overhead valve
Horsepower: 70 at 7,250 rpm
Top Speed: 125 miles per hour

high performance in terms of BMW's history. To finalize the new fairing shape, designers conducted extensive wind-tunnel testing. The addition of a pair of low bars gave the RS a more racy feel. The engine grew to 980cc, and larger 40mm Bing carburetors aided the bigger motor in maintaining a strong performance rating.

These factors increased output of the boxer twin motor to 70 horsepower at 7,250 rpm. The top speed remained at 125 miles per hour, even with the slick fairing and gear-ratio change.

The R100RS was built for four years longer than its predecessor and had 33,648 total production units, but the R100RS sold in lower numbers on an annual basis than the R90S. Since then, it has grown to be another BMW model highly desired by collectors. The cast wheels first appeared in 1977 on the bigger machines from BMW, and the example seen here wears a set of Lester rims. BMW soon offered other variants of the R100, as the platform proved itself to be chameleon-like in its ability to adapt to different riders' demands.

Did You Know?

The RS moniker refers to the German word *Rennsport*, which means "racing" and denotes machines purposefully built for that activity by BMW.

The 1977 model year saw changes to the existing lineup. BMW was still not ready to introduce any models powered by anything but the boxer. The majority of the latest entries were simply upgrades of current offerings with one fresh face joining the fray: the R80/7. It replaced the R75/7 and was positioned just beneath the R100/7.

The R100 series was the evolution result of the R90 models and carried an extra 100cc of displacement in the standard boxer format. The

1978 R100/7

Engine Type: Horizontally opposed twin
Displacement: 980cc
Years Produced: 1976–1980
Valve Configuration: Overhead valve
Horsepower: 60 at 6,500 rpm
Top Speed: 116 miles per hour

980cc engine found in the R100/7 produced 60 horsepower at 6,500 rpm and shifted through a five-speed gearbox. When the six-gallon tank

was full, the R100/7 weighed 474 pounds and was capable of reaching 116 miles per hour at its limit. A single disc brake at the front wheel and a drum at the rear slowed the speedy R100/7.

Every /7 model in 1978 could be ridden home in your choice of blue, orange, or black while the rest of the lineup sported a different choice of hues. Period magazine reviews spoke of the ongoing dependable nature of the BMW line, but excitement for it didn't measure up to that of the interest in the latest

Japanese machines trolling the streets. Riders of the Bavarian brand were well accustomed to the stable and reliable configuration of the marque, and most seemed happy to stick with the brand's format. BMWs were not considered radical, although that perception would soon change.

The R100/7 was only seen in the dealer catalogs from 1976 to 1980.

Did You Know?

In its years of production from 1976 until 1980, the R100/7 sold in numbers that exceeded 12,000 units, placing it squarely in the middle of sales figures for the period.

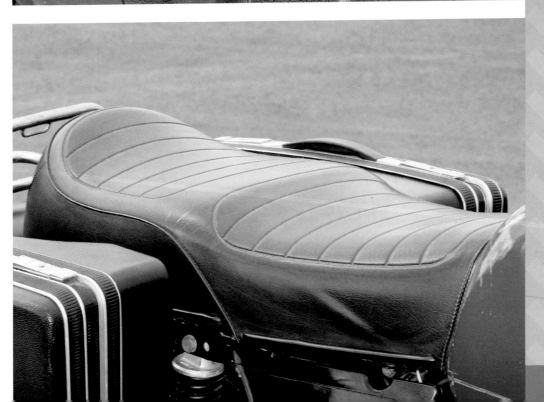

Offered as an entry-level machine, the R65 made its debut as a 1978 model. Strong sales in the first year showed BMW that there was a need for smaller and less expensive selections in the company product line. Based on the success of the R65, BMW introduced a revised edition in 1982, the R65 LS. Mechanically unchanged

1982 R65 LS

Engine Type: Horizontally opposed twin
Displacement: 649.6cc
Years Produced: 1982–1985
Valve Configuration: Overhead valve
Horsepower: 50 at 7,250 rpm
Top Speed: 108.7 miles per hour

from the R65, the LS sported a racy new fairing and integrated seat and rear cowl to set itself apart. The front wheel was wider than that found on the base R65, another unique touch.

Within the frame was the same 649.6cc boxer twin and five-speed gearbox. With a full tank of five gallons of fuel, the R65 LS weighed 456 pounds and could reach a velocity of 108.7 miles per hour. The angular contours of the front fairing reportedly reduced front-end lift by 30 percent at speed. The rear cowl was purely for style, and there was a small storage space beneath the two-person saddle.

The example seen here has the rear cowl and solo saddle from an R100RS attached, as well as Marzocchi shocks and bar end mirrors. The cylinder heads have been adapted for twin plug use, and the owner machined the brass exhaust mounting collars for ease of service. The tank bra is complete with storage pouches, making this copy a handy travel partner.

The R65 LS was sold through 1985, albeit in smaller numbers than the R65. While the R65 didn't have the smallest engine ever used in a BMW frame, the larger displacement motors remained the popular choice for a majority of the market.

Did You Know?

The angular styling of the front fairing and the graceful contours of the rear cowl of the R65 LS were once again created by the legendary designer Hans Muth. His designs bore a distinct signature that always placed them in a different league than most other motorcycles at the time. This 1982 R65 LS shared the Hans Muth stage with the Suzuki Katana of the same year.

CHAPTER 5
TRADITION AND THE BRICK

The BMW boxer engine was designed as a dependable powerplant that would survive all kinds of torture and long-distance rides. But time and the popularity of Japanese machines soon forced BMW and its trusty engine into the shadows and put the storied maker on a near-death list. Now was the time for change if BMW was to survive and thrive.

A mere revision of the twin-cylinder design wasn't an option this time. Instead BMW turned to one of its finest engineers, Josef Fritzenwenger, to craft a fresh engine. Beginning in 1977, Fritzenwenger led a small group of BMW's engineering staff to create a motor worthy of the brand. Knowing that other makers were using inline configurations for multiple-cylinder engines, Fritzenwenger decided to utilize that layout in an entirely different method.

When BMW first inline four-cylinder powerplant debuted, the inline-four engine lay on its side in the new BMW chassis, and thus it was quickly given the moniker the Flying Brick. The cylinder head poked out from the left side of the frame with the crankcase protruding from the right. The latest offering from BMW was available in three variations: the K100, K100RS, and K100RT. The K entries supplanted the previous R100 models for 1984 and received a positive response, despite their unusual appearance. While the engine was radically new by BMW standards, other features on the K models remained true to the brand. They had BMW's well-known shaft drive, but revised suspension layouts at both ends. Additional creature comforts added value and buying interest from the two-wheeled crowd.

The venerable R100s were discontinued after 1984. Compared with its brethren, the model had forged a long and fortunate life, only to be dampened near the end by competition from the Japanese.

The 980cc engine still produced adequate power for a stately BMW but suffered when compared with the ocean of new talent on the market. Delivering 67 horsepower at 7,000 rpm, the powerplant allowed the R100 to reach just

over 121 miles per hour. The wet weight of 480 pounds was a bit portly when measured against that of some of the other, lighter machines being sold. In keeping with its German heritage,

the R100 also lacked many of the comforts offered on competitors' models. It had a pair of simple gauges, a few indicator lights, but no further frills. The front end sported a pair of disc brakes, while drum brakes were at the rear, an arrangement that was considered borderline acceptable for the period. The R100s had drilled front rotors, a BMW practice that began in 1975 on the R90S.

Long-distance comfort was paramount on the R100, and the well-padded saddle was a great perch as the machine gobbled up the miles. This example has been fitted with a Hannigan STe fairing, adding to this model's comfort. When riders pushed the bike to 100 miles per hour, the speed was barely noticeable behind the full-coverage windscreen; a set of lower bars enhanced that function.

Although 1984 marked the last model year of the R100 iterations, the design would be reborn years later, as some traditionalists still preferred the boxer engine with all its quirks.

1984 R100

Engine Type: Horizontally opposed twin
Displacement: 980cc
Years Produced: 1980–1984
Valve Configuration: Overhead valve
Horsepower: 67 at 7,000 rpm
Top Speed: 121.7 miles per hour

Did You Know?

Much like the 1976 Cadillac Eldorado convertible, which claimed to be the "last one ever produced," the classic R100 design would make a return a few years down the road.

By the mid-1970s, BMW knew it needed something radically different than the company's long-lived R models. In 1977, a team of BMW engineers began efforts to create a design to move the über-traditional company forward. Several years later, in September 1984, three all-new K models were introduced in the United States. Each of the models carried a 987cc, inline

1987 K100RS

Engine Type: Inline four-cylinder
Displacement: 987cc
Years Produced: 1982–1992
Valve Configuration: Overhead valve
Horsepower: 90 at 8,000 rpm
Top Speed: 136 miles per hour

four-cylinder engine in its frame. Unlike other inline-four engines, this powerplant was placed on its side. The new K-series engines were liquid cooled as well. This layout retained the low center of gravity that older models had also had. Fuel injection replaced the previous carburetors, and a single-sided swingarm delivered power to the rear wheel.

The K100RS was aimed at the sporting crowd and came equipped with a sleek, wind-cheating fairing that provided some downforce at speed. A unique set of stripes accented the Ghost White paint. The engine cases, fork lowers, and wheels were draped in black, contrasting nicely with the glowing white bodywork. A trio of disc brakes helped to haul the K100RS down from its 136-mile-per-hour top speed. The five-speed gearbox sent the chosen ratio to a single-sided monolever swingarm. The K100RS tipped the scales at 549 pounds when topped off with the limit of 5.8 gallons of fuel.

Despite its ungainly nickname, the Flying Brick was a success for BMW. The company knew that choosing such a radical departure from its boxer engines was a risk, but buyers embraced the change. During the entire production run, from 1982 to 1992, more than 34,000 copies of the K100RS rolled off the production lines.

Did You Know?

The first inline four-cylinder engine appeared in a 1909 Pierce motorcycle. The 554cc engine delivered a handful of horsepower to the shaft drive and used a far more conventional frame than the 1912 Henderson that came a few years later.

The K1, introduced in 1989, got people talking, but it was hardly all positive. Using the 987cc engine from the K series, BMW engineers added two valves per cylinder in the K1, which boosted horsepower. The K1 had digital Motronic Brembo brakes, complete with ABS, added stopping power, and BMW's own paralever suspension on the drive end. The K100 chassis was upgraded in strength with beefier steel tubes; an altered geometry provided sharper handling.

All of these hardware updates were dressed in a rakish set of body panels that began at the near-full-coverage front fender and extended to the hinged passenger backrest. Engineers extensively tested the lines of the full-coverage fairing in a wind tunnel to learn how to reduce drag and maintain adequate wind protection for the driver. In the first few years of construction, the superbikes were finished in vivid hues accented by an enormous K1 logo in contrasting yellow. K1s built in 1991 and later wore a far more subtle cloak of muted shades at the dark end of the spectrum. The K1 set out to make a statement, and in that regard it didn't fail. Its ability to reach a top speed of 149 miles per hour didn't go without notice, but neither did the wet weight of 569 pounds.

BMW had hoped to sell more than 4,000 copies of the K1 each year, but total production failed to reach 7,000 units. Despite poor sales, the K1 showed the world that BMW was capable of building cycles that delivered more thrills. The K1 has become a highly collectible machine since its production run ended. However, prices today are nowhere near the original MSRP of $12,990.

1989

1989 & 1991 K1

Engine Type: Inline four-cylinder
Displacement: 987cc
Years Produced: 1989–1993
Valve Configuration: Overhead valve, four per cylinder
Horsepower: 100 at 8,000 rpm
Top Speed: 149 miles per hour

Did You Know?

A buyer could get a Honda CBR600, which was equally fast, lighter, and stopped in far less distance, for about a third of the cost of a new BMW K1.

1989

1989

1989

1989

1991

The Paris–Dakar endurance race is known to be one of the toughest challenges a motorcycle rider can face. In BMW's past, riders aboard the storied brand racked up four victories in the race, bringing renown to the brand.

In 1990, BMW launched the R100GS/Paris Dakar, and by all appearances it was a true race machine for on- and off-road use. Before the

1990 R100GS/PARIS DAKAR

Engine Type: Horizontally opposed twin
Displacement: 980cc
Years Produced: 1988–1995
Valve Configuration: Overhead valve
Horsepower: 60 at 6,500 rpm
Top Speed: 111 miles per hour

official PD edition appeared, all of the same components on it were available at your local BMW dealer. The PD designation wasn't used until BMW gained legal use of the Paris–Dakar name. The GS designation referred to the Gelände Sport Enduro category.

The R100GS/Paris Dakar was laden with features befitting a heavy-duty off-road machine, including the 9.5-gallon fuel tank, heated grips, a Brembo front brake, and a Marzocchi fork. The model had a five-speed gearbox and 34mm Bing carburetors. Full of fuel, the R100GS/Paris Dakar weighed 520 pounds and provided 60-horsepower output. BMW's own paralever suspension was installed at the tail end, along with a drum brake. The front wheel held a drilled disc brake.

Protective gear included the heavy-duty skid plate beneath the engine, hand guards, and a headlight cage. The solo saddle is well padded, and the windscreen does what it can to deflect flying debris. A large luggage rack is joined by a set of hard-sided saddlebags, allowing the rider storage space to endure the full length of the race.

The first BMW cycles built for the race appeared in 1981. The added displacement of the R100GS was in response to demand for more power.

Did You Know?

The Paris–Dakar rally covers more than 6,000 miles and takes two weeks to complete. Cars and motorcycles have participated for decades, and the BMW entries have been very competitive in the race.

The R1100RS was the culmination of BMW's efforts over the previous 70 years. While three- and four-cylinder models now were showcased in BMW dealerships, the true enthusiast always preferred the boxer-twin layout.

The R1100RS carried a traditional horizontally opposed twin in its frame but was now delivered with a bevy of go-fast gear. The heads were now four-valve affairs, and fuel was meted out using Bosch Motronic MA 2.2 fuel

injection. The cylinder heads also featured the latest design that used oil circulating through each for improved cooling versus the "airhead" design that had been used since the first days of the brand. A five-speed gearbox sent the power to the paralever rear end. The front forks now featured the telelever system, created by BMW to provide enhanced control and comfort to the rider and passenger.

Slowing the R1100RS down from its 133-mile-per-hour top speed was a triple set of disc brakes, with two on the front wheel. For safer stops, the front discs were also paired with ABS. With its capacity of 6.07 gallons in the fuel tank, the R1100RS had a curb weight of 527 pounds. Wrapped around all of the latest technology was a full-coverage fairing that was integrated into the tail section in a seamless flow. The single-sided swingarm was part of the paralever suspension that removed any trace of "lift" under acceleration or when bringing the R1100RS to a halt. A tidy bank of instruments was behind the windscreen, which also protected the rider from the elements.

1994 R1100RS

Engine Type: Horizontally opposed twin
Displacement: 1,085cc
Years Produced: 1993–2001
Valve Configuration: Overhead valve, four per cylinder
Horsepower: 90 at 7,250 rpm
Top Speed: 133 miles per hour

Did You Know?
The application of the "oilhead" system served two different types of BMW fans. There was the faction who missed the beloved air-cooled boxer engine and those who appreciated the improved cooling that didn't step too far away from the original design.

There will always be a demand for motorcycles capable of swallowing 1,000 miles in a day. Early examples designed to meet that demand were little more than large displacement models with saddlebags added. BMW's own R100RT was well known for its high-mile abilities, but at that stage, the world of electronics was only a dream.

1999 K1200LT

Engine Type: Inline-four
Displacement: 1,171cc
Years Produced: 1999–2007
Valve Configuration: Overhead valve, four per cylinder
Horsepower: 98 at 6,750 rpm
Top Speed: 122 miles per hour

The K1200LT and the LT designation debuted in 1999. LT stood for Luxus Tourer, or Luxury Tourer in US versions. The LT was sold in three trim levels, each with more features than the last. The top end was the Custom and offered the rider and passenger every feature known to man: a six-CD changer, heated grips and seats, onboard computer to monitor progress, cruise control, and a few touches of chrome.

All of this opulence came at a price both in dollars and weight. When the 6.18-gallon tank was full, the K1200LT weighed in at 833 pounds. BMW was aware of the tonnage and installed an 1,171cc, inline-four engine with Bosch Motronic MA 2.4 fuel injection. The result of this mix delivered 98 ponies at 6,750 rpm and propelled the K1200LT to a speed of 122 miles per hour. Bringing the behemoth to a halt was the duty of the three floating rotors and four-piston Brembo calipers.

As mentioned, the cost to bring a K1200LT home wasn't a bargain, but the equipment included justified nearly every dime of the $16,900 to $18,900 (the price based on the trim level you selected). Overall, the K1200LT had an impressive powerplant and a long list of comforts.

Did You Know?

Honda's Gold Wing was a long-distance mount that made its debut in 1975. It would be five years until it had a fairing and saddlebags. Electronic trickery would follow within a few years, making the GL an early example of what a touring machine could be.

VOLUME

TP
MUTE

BMW had long sold motorcycles with one-, two-, three-, and four-cylinder engines, so the use of the one-jug motor in the F650 was not a shock. Perhaps it's hard to believe that the engine was a Rotax product, but it's true nonetheless. More unusual was the use of a chain for the final drive, the first ever for the Bavarian builder. From the beginning, the F650 was intended as an entry-level BMW, and the MSRP for a 2000 model was "only" $7,900.

For that paltry fee, you rode home on a nimble machine that weighed 421 pounds with a full tank (4.62 gallons) and delivered almost 48 horsepower. The single-cylinder was water-cooled and sipped through a 43mm

fuel-injection body. The exhaust canister was mounted high on the chassis, an indication of its off-road potential. Designed as a machine capable of both on- and off-road use, the F650 didn't dazzle at either but still delivered. Top speed was not its strong suit; it was listed as 101 miles per hour. A compact windscreen did its best to shield the rider from the wind and elements. The F650 had a basic array of gauges behind that windscreen.

The F650 made its debut in Europe as a 1993 model and was released in the United States in 1997. Originally built by Aprilia using the Rotax engine, it would later be assembled by BMW. As time marched on, different variations of the base F650 Funduro were offered. The deviations were largely cosmetic but worked better when the terrain got rough. In scrambler fashion, the F650 could be ridden on the street and trails as long as you didn't expect miracles doing either. Described as a competent machine by period magazines, it provided enough range and comfort to appeal to first-time buyers of the legendary brand. The last year F650s were seen at dealers was 2007, but they now pop up periodically at swap meets and on eBay.

2000 F650

Engine Type: Single-cylinder, four-stroke
Displacement: 652cc
Years Produced: 1993–2007
Valve Configuration: Dual overhead cam
Horsepower: 47.59 at 6,500 rpm
Top Speed: 101 miles per hour

Did You Know?

BMW was the only motorcycle manufacturer to use nothing but shaft drives for 70 years before turning to a drive chain. The F650 was intended for use on- and off-road and was sold at a lower price point than any other model in the BMW catalog. A final drive chain was less expensive and lighter weight than the shaft-drive assembly, thus killing two birds with one stone.

CHAPTER 6
A NEW CENTURY AND FRESH IDEAS

The new century arrived, and despite dire predictions, everyone avoided the pitfalls of Y2K. BMW had been expanding the scope of its model lineup since 1983. Now it was releasing upgraded K models that were a stark contrast to the previous decade's offerings, and most enthusiasts applauded the excitement they delivered. Also, BMW focused on making derivations on a few machines, a trend the company kept building on.

In an attempt to build a true superbike, BMW introduced the K1, and it received mostly positive reviews. Perhaps more than the new hardware it showed, it told the world that BMW was willing to step outside its strictly traditional lineup.

Following in the footsteps of the K1 came a steady stream of high-end touring models. Equipped with variations of the original K-series engine and draped with features and finery, they quickly reached the pinnacle of motorcycle design. Heated grips and seats were joined by electronic controls that rivaled the early space flights. Riders who sought the best that life had to offer welcomed these touring bikes.

Another direction BMW pursued was the development of sportbikes. Prior models had been sporty, but none stepped as deeply into that realm as the S1000 did. The series featured cutting-edge performance wrapped in svelte bodywork, with handling and braking on par with the best the racing world had to offer. The technology impressed the motorcycle world in ways not seen since 1969.

With BMW having broken the barrier to more avant-garde creations, I, for one, am looking forward to what the engineers at the company have to show us in the years to come. After the K1 and S1000RR, there are no limits to what may be rolled out next.

Even before the new century appeared, BMW fans had seen a hint of how daring the manufacturer had become when it came to motorcycle designs. The creation of the K motor sent chills down the spines of traditional BMW riders but drew an entirely new crop of riders who were drawn to the Flying Brick. The engine had already been used in several displacements by 2000, and that trend would continue.

Touring models also had been in the BMW repertoire for years, but the latest crop would employ a rash of electronic toys to accent the performance of the K powerplants. The K1200GT first appeared as a 2003 model.

It rode into the sport-touring category and gained respect upon its release. Completely hidden behind the swooping bodywork was a 1,157cc example of the K motor. The water-cooled, inline four-cylinder produced 130.5 horsepower and carried six speeds in the gearbox. A top speed of 149.75 miles per hour was on tap, and a trio of disc brakes hauled it back to stop.

Among the features that were standard on the K1200GT were an adjustable saddle, ABS braking, and hard-sided luggage. Add-ons such as heated grips and seat, on-board computer, and automatic stability control further gained the respect of the most demanding riders. When adding a full tank of fuel (5.42 gallons), the K1200GT had a curb weight of 661 pounds.

The evolution of BMW's big touring models continued as years went by. In 2008, K1300GT came out, sending the K1200GT packing. The K1300GT brought more of everything, as riders continued to demand additional features and power from their luxury machines.

2004 K1200GT

Engine Type: Inline four-cylinder
Displacement: 1,157cc
Years Produced: 2003–2008
Valve Configuration: Dual overhead valve, four per cylinder
Horsepower: 130.5 at 8,750 rpm
Top Speed: 149.75 miles per hour

Did You Know?

The engine in the K1200GT was the same as that used in a K1200S, which earned a world record in its class for top speed in 2005. The K1200S was ridden to a velocity of 173.57 miles per hour at the Bonneville Salt Flats in Utah.

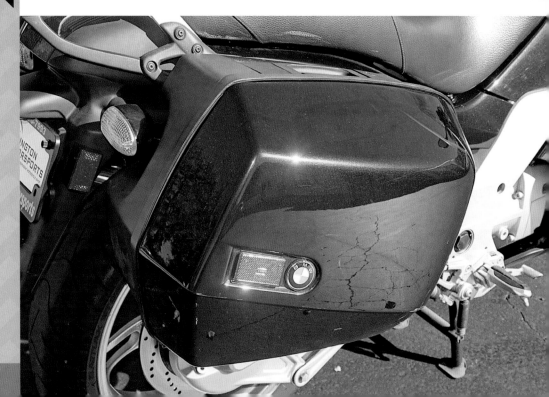

In 2005, the final Boxer Cup race was held at Daytona International Speedway. As in the previous year, the BMW Boxer Cup R1100S was the model used. The race editions were modified for the ultimate performance on the track, and the Replica mirrored the race version closely. The Replica derived from the R1100S made its debut as a 2003 edition.

The R1100S had a 1,085cc motor that produced 98 horsepower at 7,500 rpm. A twin-spark head could be found on both cylinders. A six-speed gearbox added a measure of options to the serious rider. The R1100S motor was overshadowed by some of its sibling's engines but was a competent powerplant, well suited for racing. The balance of output and

delivery made the Replica a fast, yet pleasant, mount for the eager rider. The R1100RS had no radical level of power, nor a frightening delivery of the ponies, on tap. Period publications said as much but still lauded the BMW despite its less-than-stellar performance.

The chassis on the Replica was enhanced and raised 12mm to provide added ground

clearance. The seat height was a lofty 33.9 inches. Front fork tubes were borrowed from the R1150GS to boost stiffness and enhance handling. A pair of 12.6-inch floating brake rotors was on the back, as well as four-piston calipers. At the tail end was a single floating rotor of 10.9 inches with a two-piston caliper.

The sweeping graphics used on the Boxer Cup Replica made a bold statement, and the under tail–mounted exhaust continued that theme. The fuel tank held 4.7 gallons and provided plenty of time in the saddle between refueling. Based on a racing model, the R1100S wasn't flush with creature-comfort features, but there was a long list of available upgrades to really improve that status.

The Boxer Cup event was short lived but did give a select few riders an opportunity to experience the thrills that racing on a track offered.

2005 R1100S BOXER CUP REPLICA

Engine Type: Horizontally opposed twin
Displacement: 1,085cc
Years Produced: 2003–2005
Valve Configuration: Overhead valve
Horsepower: 98 at 7,500 rpm
Top Speed: 141 miles per hour

Did You Know?

The Boxer Cup was held at the Daytona International Speedway. First open in 1959, the two-and-a-half-mile circuit has been the home of the annual Daytona 500 every year since its inception. Other annual races include the Daytona 200, which kicks off the AMA Superbike series.

The next salvo that BMW fired in the sportbike war was the K1200S. First seen as a 2004 model, the latest effort delivered high horsepower mated to comfort, and it quickly rose through the ranks. The K1200S was the culmination of five years of design aimed to deliver the most competent BMW sportbike the world had ever seen. The sportbike arena was cluttered with competing machines at the time, including the Honda Blackbird and Suzuki Hayabusa, and BMW wanted a solid sportbike offering of its own.

2006 K1200S WITH ABS

Engine Type: Inline four-cylinder
Displacement: 1,157cc
Years Produced: 2004–2012
Valve Configuration: Overhead valve, four per cylinder
Horsepower: 167 at 10,250 rpm
Top Speed: 165 miles per hour

The K1200S had a 1,157cc, inline four-cylinder engine placed in its frame at a rakish 55-degree angle. This design provided the

rider with a lower center of gravity, as well as a long wheelbase that added comfort when on the open road. Horsepower was listed as 167 at 10,250 rpm, so the K1200S was the most powerful model in BMW's history. The "S" designation hearkened back to the days of the R90S, which debuted in 1973 and also showed BMW meant business.

The K1200S was not svelte or petite, but with a top speed of 165 miles per hour, it was hard to tell as it rocketed past. The 62-inch wheelbase was nearly five inches longer than any of the competition, and when fueled up, the K1200S tipped the scales at 546.7 pounds. A six-speed gearbox provided ample gear choices to meet riders' demands, as did the four valves per cylinder. The model also had electronic fuel injection and a trio of disc brakes; antilock ABS was offered as an option.

Period magazine reviews lauded the fresh design from BMW, although the nearly $20,000 MSRP (when fully equipped) did not elude their attention. A high price doesn't always equal results, but in the case of the BMW, buyers got what they paid for. The K1200S screamed power and control, and the build quality was a Bavarian form of art.

Did You Know?

When BMW designed the K1200S, the company wanted it to be the machine to strike death to the Honda Blackbird and the Suzuki Hayabusa. The Hayabusa was named for the fastest falcon on record, and its premier colors were chosen to mimic the famed bird in soft tones of copper and silver.

Following in the muddy tire tracks of the R1150GS, the R1200GS first appeared as a 2004 model. The new edition lost 66 pounds and gained 19 horsepower over its predecessor. For the 2008 version, another five ponies were on tap and antilock braking was added. BMW's boxer twin-cylinder engine was used and now displaced 1,170cc.

2008 R1200GS

Engine Type: Horizontally opposed twin
Displacement: 1,170cc
Years Produced: 2004–2012
Valve Configuration: Overhead valve, four per cylinder
Horsepower: 105 at 7,500 rpm
Top Speed: 124 miles per hour

With an intended purpose of riding on- and off-road, the suspension travel was generous and the tire-tread patterns suited the same needs. A BMW-designed suspension was used at both ends: telelever in the front and paralever out back. Options that added to the useful nature of the layout included automatic stability control and a traction control system.

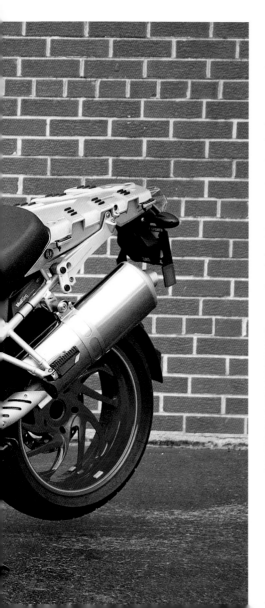

The R1200GS had a pair of disc brakes with four-piston calipers at the front. The tail end had a third disc with a dual-piston caliper. As per the norm, a six-speed gearbox was installed. When the 5.3-gallon fuel tank was full, the R1200GS weighed in at 496 pounds.

Styling leaned toward the off-road aspects with plenty of clearance between the tires and fenders. A rugged luggage rack rode above the rear fender, and skid plates helped to protect the chassis and powertrain. The factory wheels on this example have been replaced with a set borrowed from a 1200 Sport model. Both hoops measure 17 inches in diameter, supplanting the original 19-inch versions. Handling and control were enhanced with this upgrade, traits the bike's owner enjoys. The owner also removed the lower skid plate and a section of the seat and rack to save weight.

Production of the R1200GS ran through 2012 and claimed a top seat on BMW's sales hierarchy. The standard GS was also sold in an Adventure and Special Edition version, giving buyers more reasons to buy and ride wherever they chose.

Did You Know?

While the R1200GS series was a very popular seller, it endured nine different safety recalls. Nearly every facet of the machine was affected at one point, starting with front brakes and ABS. The fuel pump, throttle cable, and final drive were also tended to.

In BMW's history, the Bavarian company has introduced a bevy of dependable and traditional models, but every once in a great while, BMW takes a ride on the wild side. The K1 was the earliest and the R nineT is the latest. Beginning in 2008, the staid firm delivered a variety of machines that defied BMW's own heritage. A superbike, dirt bike, and six-cylinder mega touring model were seen along with scooters.

The R nineT is a bit more mild compared with some of BMW's most recent creations, and it was the result of a collaboration of several builders of custom cycles. It may have been timid for those custom builders, but for BMW, it still was a radical departure. The end result is more dark-alley bruiser than elegant enthusiast, but it has proven to be a runaway success.

Compared with the dramatic design, the powertrain remains semitraditional with a boxer-twin motor at the helm. Displacing 1,170cc and cooled with air and oil, it produces 110 horsepower at 7,750 rpm. A pair of conical exhaust canisters are found on the left side of the chassis, and they feature internal baffles that can be removed far more easily than in the past. That change brings some added snarl to the R nineT equation. If a buyer wants to turn an R nineT into more of a café racer, a high level of personal items can be purchased through the BMW catalog. The R nineT seen here wears a number of these products and provides the owner with a high degree of pride.

When fully fueled, the R nineT weighs 489. Its standard seat can carry two adults in style, while this example wears an aluminum cowl that turns it into a solo mount. Features and output make the R nineT a truly unique machine, and buyers are flocking to the showrooms to ride one home.

2014 R NINET

Engine Type: Horizontally opposed twin
Displacement: 1,170cc
Years Produced: 2014 to present
Valve Configuration: Overhead valve, four per cylinder
Horsepower: 110 at 7,750 rpm
Top Speed: More than 125 miles per hour

Did You Know?

The shocking arrival of the R nineT came as a surprise to traditional BMW buyers, but the rogue design brought customers flocking. Some dealers had buyers waiting more than six months before another R nineT was delivered.

Illinois 06-15

BMW

Only in recent years has BMW released truly high-performance models. The K1 was an early attempt at a sport-touring offering, but the S1000R and RR ramped up every facet of that machine. The S1000RR was actually BMW's entrant into the hotly contested World Superbike class that made its debut in 2008. In order to race the RR, BMW had to build 1,000 copies to be sold for street use. Obviously the racing version took every aspect to the highest degree, but the tamer street-legal version was no slouch.

2014 S1000RR

Engine Type: Inline four-cylinder
Displacement: 999cc
Years Produced: 2008 to present
Valve Configuration: Overhead valve, four per cylinder
Horsepower: 193 at 13,000 rpm
Top Speed: More than 125 miles per hour

Nestled in the alloy perimeter frame is a 999cc, inline four-cylinder powerplant that puts 193 horsepower in the rider's grip. The most obvious change seen on the S1000RR was the use of a final chain drive. BMW had long forged its reputation using nothing but shaft drive, but that configuration ate up horsepower. To race and win, the S1000RR needed to retain every spare ounce of power. On duty to control all of this power was standard traction control.

Included in the go-fast equation were titanium valves (four per cylinder), floating rotor brakes with race ABS, and a six-speed gearbox. The two-sided swingarm and chassis were formed using an aluminum alloy for stiffness and less weight. When topped off with 4.6 gallons of fuel, the S1000RR tipped the scales at only 449 pounds. An inverted front fork added rigidity and aided handling. Four-piston calipers squeezed a set of 12.6-inch floating brake rotors.

First introduced in February of 2008, the road-going version of the S1000RR is still gaining new riders every year. The limited production keeps the interest level high but rewards those patient buyers with a machine worthy of the wait.

Did You Know?

As a newcomer to the World Superbike arena, BMW wasn't expecting to win at the first races. By employing Troy Corser and Ruben Xaus as the pilots for the series, BMW certainly tipped the scales in its favor. Corser pushed the all-new machine to an eighth-place finish at its first foray into the SBK universe.

The first BMW HP series began in 2005 with a line of super sport entries powered by a twin-cylinder engine. The HP stands for high performance, and the debut of the HP4 in 2012 showed the world what the legendary motorcycle builder could do. Based on the potent S1000RR, the HP4 adds more of everything and loses weight in the process. With a full tank of fuel, the HP4 weighs a scant 439 pounds. The same output of 193 horsepower at 13,000 rpm was still on hand, propelling the latest rocket to new levels.

A big reason for the reduced weight was the carbon fiber bodywork, which, because of its superior stiffness and light weight, is used on race car chassis across the globe. The paint scheme is applied to expose a few subtle sections of the aerospace material's weave.

The advantage of carbon fiber is not lost when applied to a cycle with nearly 200 ponies under its cloak. Beneath the exotic skin, the BMW features an alloy chassis that employs the engine as a stressed member.

The engine is a 999cc powerhouse that feeds through 48mm throttle bodies. The dual overhead cam motor features four valves per cylinder, and the entire arrangement is liquid cooled. The HP4 has a final drive by chain.

Several other features on the HP4 are carried over from the S1000RR, including an inverted front fork and a pair of floating brake rotors up front. Another smaller rotor is found at the rear wheel. A six-speed gearbox has become a common item on today's motorcycles at nearly every level of performance.

The HP4 can be ridden on the street or taken to the track with few modifications needed. The HP4 is an exclusive and fairly rare beast. Each one carries a unique HP4 serial number on the upper triple clamp, telling the world of its scarcity. Keeping the rider informed of his velocity is an array of gauges that blends analog and digital information that can be absorbed at a glance. All of that hides behind a carefully sculpted fairing that is beautiful and as aerodynamic as a modern fighter jet.

2014 HP4

Engine Type: Inline four-cylinder
Displacement: 999cc
Years Produced: 2012 to 2014
Valve Configuration: Overhead valve, four per cylinder
Horsepower: 193 at 13,000 rpm
Top Speed: In excess of 125 miles per hour

Did You Know?

The information found on any of today's sport models from BMW lists top speed as "over 125 MPH" but offers no actual figures. This trick hearkens back to the early days of Rolls-Royce automobiles, when the company listed horsepower as "adequate," with no further data provided.

On a visit to the sales floor of my local BMW dealer, I was taken aback at the size and unusual shapes of the C650GT. But why? Although I'm a fan of most things two-wheeled, the world of scooters remains on the outer edges of my interest, on a good day.

Make no mistake, the BMW C650GT and C600 Sport models are built using the highest quality of materials found in today's market.

Both are chock-full of features and can travel at speeds in excess of 100 miles per hour. When fully fueled, the C650GT tips the scales at a hefty 575 pounds. That figure exceeds most of the other models in the BMW catalog. The wheelbase is also a gigantic 62.6 inches, which makes it nearly three-fourths of an inch longer than the K1200GT.

Powering this mini-behemoth is a parallel twin-cylinder engine that displaces 647cc and puts out 60 horsepower at 7,500 rpm. The top speed is claimed to be 109 miles per hour, and an automatic gearbox provides easy twist-and-go performance. The step-through configuration permits easy access for nearly anyone and has been a crucial element of scooter design for decades. BMW considered the term "scooter" to be old school and opted for "urban mobility vehicle" instead.

The design and execution of the UMV are typical BMW, but the weight and cost (MSRP $10,000) don't seem to apply to an actual motorcycle product. The C650GT comes complete with enough storage for running casual errands or getting a person to and from work with any required gear. And since it can achieve speeds in excess of 100 miles per hour, it will get you there in a timely fashion.

The popularity of scooters or UMVs in the United States has always paled in comparison to their popularity in European and Asian markets. Despite my misgivings on the C650GT, I'm certain it will gain a few fans here in the United States. With a fuel-mileage rating of 50 miles per gallon, it can travel more than 200 miles between refills, which should reduce the sting of the high cost of entry and weight.

2014 C650GT URBAN MOBILITY VEHICLE

Engine Type: Parallel twin-cylinder
Displacement: 647cc
Years Produced: 2013–2014
Valve Configuration: Overhead valve, four per cylinder
Horsepower: 60 at 7,500 rpm
Top Speed: 109 miles per hour

Did You Know?

The Honda C100 was not the first step-through design used, but Honda's "You meet the nicest people on a Honda" ad campaign showed the world a new way to get around in style. European-branded scooters came years before the Honda, and many are still heavily used today.